EXPLORING
SATURN

By Mary Austen

KidHaven
PUBLISHING

Published in 2018 by
KidHaven Publishing, an Imprint of Greenhaven Publishing, LLC
353 3rd Avenue
Suite 255
New York, NY 10010

Designer: Deanna Paternostro
Editor: Vanessa Oswald

Photo credits: Cover, back cover Vadim Sadovski/Shutterstock.com; p. 5 Tanya Zima/ Shutterstock.com; pp. 6–7 abcjan/Shutterstock.com; p. 7 (inset) My Portfolio/Shutterstock.com; p. 9 Aphelleon/Shutterstock.com; p. 11 SkyPics Studio/Shutterstock.com; p. 13 Nostalgia for Infinity/ Shutterstock.com; p. 15 (main) Science & Society Picture Library/Contributor/SSPL/Getty Images; p. 15 (inset) Tony Wills/Wikimedia Commons; p. 17 Johan-Swanepoel/Shutterstock.com; p. 19 (main) Comstock Images/Getty Images; p. 19 (inset) Tristan3D/Shutterstock.com; p. 21 Space Frontiers/Stringer/Archive Photos/Getty Images.

Cataloging-in-Publication Data

Names: Austen, Mary.
Title: Exploring Saturn / Mary Austen.
Description: New York : KidHaven Publishing, 2018. | Series: Journey through our solar system | Includes index.
Identifiers: ISBN 9781534522886 (pbk.) | 9781534522824 (library bound) | ISBN 9781534522541 (6 pack) | ISBN 9781534522633 (ebook)
Subjects: LCSH: Saturn (Planet)–Juvenile literature.
Classification: LCC QB671.A93 2018 | DDC 523.46–dc23
Printed in the United States of America

CPSIA compliance information: Batch #BS17KL: For further information contact Greenhaven Publishing LLC, New York, New York at 1-844-317-7404.

Please visit our website, www.greenhavenpublishing.com. For a free color catalog of all our high-quality books, call toll free 1-844-317-7404 or fax 1-844-317-7405.

CONTENTS

THE PLANET OF RINGS

Saturn is the second-largest planet in our **solar system**. It's the sixth planet from the sun. Saturn is known for the rings around it.

Saturn

Saturn is the farthest planet
that can be seen in the night
sky with the human eye.

Just like all the other planets, Saturn **orbits** the sun. It takes 29.5 Earth years to go around the sun once.

However, Saturn spins much more quickly than Earth. It only takes 10.5 hours to make one **rotation**.

Saturn's orbit, or path, around the sun is shown here.

GIANT PLANET OF GAS

Saturn is called a gas giant. It's circled by thick clouds made up of mostly **hydrogen**. The gas giants—Jupiter, Saturn, Uranus, and Neptune—don't have solid ground.

Saturn's color comes from **ammonia** in its **atmosphere**.

THE LAYERS OF SATURN

Beneath Saturn's atmosphere is a **layer** of liquid hydrogen and **helium**. The center of the planet, known as the core, is made of hot iron and rock.

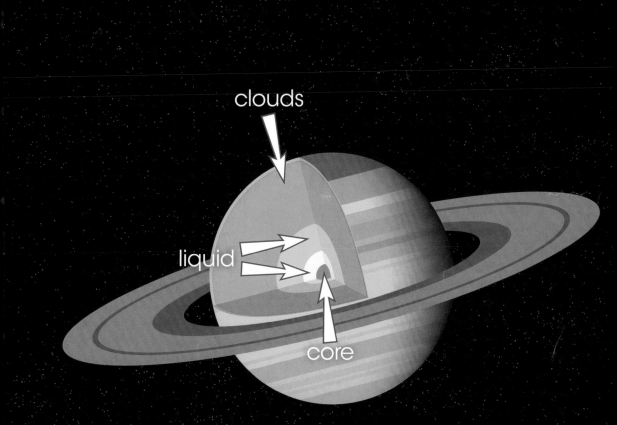

clouds

liquid

core

Shown here are Saturn's layers.

THE RINGS OF SATURN

Saturn has floating rings that circle the planet. These rings orbit Saturn just like Saturn orbits the sun.

Saturn has very thin rings that are thousands of miles wide.

Saturn's rings

Saturn's rings are made up of mostly ice and rocks. Scientists believe the rings were formed from **asteroids** that broke apart before reaching the planet.

Ice chunks make up Saturn's rings.

ice chunks

Shown here is a close-up photograph of Saturn's rings.

15

SATURN'S MOONS

Saturn has more than 62 moons of different sizes. The planet's smallest moon is 0.33 mile (0.5 km) wide, and its biggest moon is half the size of Earth.

Scientists believe Saturn could have many more moons that haven't been discovered yet.

Titan is Saturn's largest moon. It's the second-largest moon in the whole solar system and is made of mostly rock and ice. The only moon larger is Jupiter's moon Ganymede (GA-nih-meed).

Titan is the only moon that has clouds.

Titan

moons

moons

moon

19

GETTING TO KNOW SATURN

Scientists have sent **probes** to study Saturn. In 1979, the *Pioneer 11* became the first probe to reach Saturn. This probe discovered the planet's outer rings. Other probes have also been sent to teach us about the ringed planet.

The *Cassini-Huygens* spacecraft has been studying Saturn since 2004. It even landed on Titan!

Pioneer 11 probe

GLOSSARY

ammonia: A colorless gas with a strong smell.

asteroid: A large rock in space left over from the start of the solar system.

atmosphere: Gases in the air around a planet.

helium: The second lightest gas in the solar system.

hydrogen: The lightest gas in the solar system.

layer: One part of something lying over or under another.

orbit: To travel in a circle or oval around something.

probe: A vehicle that sends information about an object in space back to Earth.

rotation: The act of an object turning in a circle.

solar system: The sun and all the space objects that orbit it, including planets and their moons.

FOR MORE INFORMATION

Websites

NASA Space Place: All About Saturn
spaceplace.nasa.gov/all-about-saturn/en/
NASA provides readers with cool pictures of and information about Saturn.

National Geographic Kids: Mission to Saturn
kids.nationalgeographic.com/explore/space/ mission-to-saturn/#saturn-planet.jpg
This website includes fun facts about Saturn.

Books

Bloom, J.P. *Saturn*. Minneapolis, MN: Abdo Kids, 2015.

Glaser, Chaya. *Saturn: Amazing Rings*. New York, NY: Bearport Publishing, 2015.

Radomski, Kassandra. *The Secrets of Saturn*. North Mankato, MN: Capstone Press, 2016.

INDEX